Water Basin

Water Basin

DAVINA ALLISON

RESOURCE *Publications* • Eugene, Oregon

WATER BASIN

Resource Publications
An Imprint of Wipf and Stock Publishers
199 W. 8th Ave., Suite 3
Eugene, OR 97401

www.wipfandstock.com

PAPERBACK ISBN: 979-8-3852-7234-1
HARDCOVER ISBN: 979-8-3852-7235-8
EBOOK ISBN: 979-8-3852-7236-5
VERSION NUMBER 01/26/26

For my brilliant children, now grown

I acknowledge the Traditional Owners of Country throughout Australia. I pay my respects to Elders past, present, and emerging.

Contents

Acknowledgments

I would like to thank my family and friends for making my personal living rich. These poems were written during the final year of my son's secondary schooling, while he was studying for his ATAR. Love, congratulations. 98.1.

Thank you so much to Mel for years of counter-cultural exemplarity, and love.

I am also grateful for the many thinkers and writers of the Church whose work is water.

Thank you to the excellent team at Wipf and Stock.

Another Night

I left notes
under the vase
with the hand-painted

cornflowers,

a fluted lip
You always had
something in it, depending
on the time of year, jasmine

It was cold today.
It started to rain
while I was walking home
through the fields.

Sunday

a page marked by
a field marigold

one night
when you couldn't sleep,
which you found
flowering.

Dipped a brush in water

the frankincense you wear

Tonight you are at your desk
where you have
a photo of me
looking back
at you from the water

a silver dish
with a curved handle.

You close the window
wonder if the marigolds need watering

Wind Bell

you paint
the water flowers
we saw
yesterday

your back to the window
which opens
onto the veranda where
I pot roses

your hair pinned up

brushstroke

Years ago
you sent me a book
wrapped in finely

woven muslin

which I held in my hands,
up to the light

a water tank, overgrown

What are you painting

you reading, a birch in the window

picking handfuls of mint,
washing your hands
Leaning over to turn off the tap

when you were painting river birds

in the light
coming through
a window,
a lemon tree outside

your hair up,
pearl earrings

A Storm all Night

he thinks of you

planting violets
separating
the seedlings with
your hands, watering them

Sunday, after cutting a rose

When you say, love

I am at the window, for a moment
looking out
through the trees

a mussel shell in his hand

it's winter now

I sketch sometimes
if there is enough light

when
you leant forward to
write marigolds
On an envelope

the flowers you wanted

tonight I watched a storm
from our bed
it reminded me of

the night
you
walked to the edge
of the water
in your nightie

Sunday Afternoon

when we met
it was late spring

the roses are beautiful
have you seen the bird paintings

showed me
a painting of a bird
on a fence
with a blue tail

Room with Muslin Curtains

We lie awake in a storm

Do you remember when I asked you to marry me

you were looking for
a bird, still in the water,
and it started to rain

And the Sea

you prune the orange tree, shower

in the margin
Storms this morning

fullness of time

Each day
the sound of birds

when I'm in the garden
turning on the tap to fill
the watering can.

sometimes rain

It will be Winter

asleep in our bed
above you
paintings

outside orange flowers where they fell

this morning

you, love,
Your shirt undone,
reading
and by our bed

a drawing of a mulberry tree

you wash a paintbrush in water

where violets dry on the sill

I wanted to remind you
of the long winter
we fell in love
When we would wake early

desire

you said you loved how
delicate
they are
when we saw them
among water grass

a map of the river

the night
you walked through the rain
to bring me violets

I used to pick them
where they grew
by the water tank

for my dresser which had a cloth

with birds hand-stitched

he untangles a net made of silk

the water is clear
there's still an hour before dark

my love looking up
at the sound of a bird

moving a pot into the sun

Morning

He sits in the garden thinking of his love

her bed unmade,
standing
at the window

light of a candle

He touches the bangle on my wrist

it was wrapped in silk, pale blue embroidery

it was raining
so we stayed
in the library,
read to each other

left water in the basin

When you would write to me
come tonight it's meant to rain.
Love I can't sleep

lie awake
when you potted seedlings

pour water

You look up from your book,
say good morning

tell me about the light

on my worktable
note paper
where you’ve painted a heron

Alabaster Bowl for Water

Outside the hay is being cut

I was waiting for you

I'd leave a note,
if the orange tree is in flower

open the window
I'll go inland for the iris
they say
grows

after rain

the smell of burning candles

When you can't sleep
you like to be near me

leave notes,
when to plant

a primacy of the intellect

for my senior English class, 2024–2025, Bright Stars

those white flowers
open
under a painting
of the sea

they don't flower for long

after rain which brings the birds

Letter, One Winter Night

the silk thread
I sent you
reminds me of the violets
growing
wild
over the graves
when we sheltered from the rain.
We picked handfuls
you started a watercolour

are they true

for you
a silk panel

it's like the painting we saw

At this Hour

It's raining again. I turn off the light

think of you
standing in the shallows

you're there for a pearl shell

when you gave it to me,
you said you wanted me to have
a shell like the one
on your desk

where you keep a fine vase

Insights

the first time
I saw you
you were standing before a painting
of a butterfly
above a lemon

did you know there's a
wild rose in the back field

Water Basin

you like to sit by
a window
lilies in a blue glass jar
which you fill
at the tap

underneath there are violets

while there is time

the orange trees

are almost ready to flower,
the days are mild

his hands smell of soil, tobacco

Jasmine, Back Fence

rain filling the tank woke me

flowers on the bedside tonight

When you were away, you would send
various flowers
for the seeds,

a cut geranium.

Aesthetic Values

You wake before me

write on blue note paper.

I wanted to see the birds
the marigolds
growing there

Beethoven on low, rain

when you come in through
the front gate
there's a climbing rose
which I was going to prune back

the birch tree I planted as a sapling

My Love

you are already up,
With your notebook, sketching
a bird on
a mooring
the background, water

a painting of a small bird

I have cotton worked in silk
which I bought once
when I couldn't
sleep, they were unloading

the night boats

today you marry me

violets
in a porcelain dish
so you can paint them, the first of winter

and the window, open
to morning

www.ingramcontent.com/pod-product-compliance
Lightning Source LLC
LaVergne TN
LVHW010546100826
845148LV00013B/2630

* 9 7 9 8 3 8 5 2 7 2 3 4 1 *